Mary Tyler Cheek

THE RESURRECTION AND THE LIFE

THE RESURRECTIO

ND THE LIFE

Leslie D. Weatherhead

YORK : NASHVILLE : ABINGDON-COKESBURY PRESS

THE RESURRECTION AND THE LIFE

Library of Congress Catalog Card Number: 52-11309

C

SET UP, PRINTED, AND BOUND BY THE PARTHENON PRESS AT NASHVILLE, TENNESSEE, UNITED STATES OF AMERICA

CONTENTS

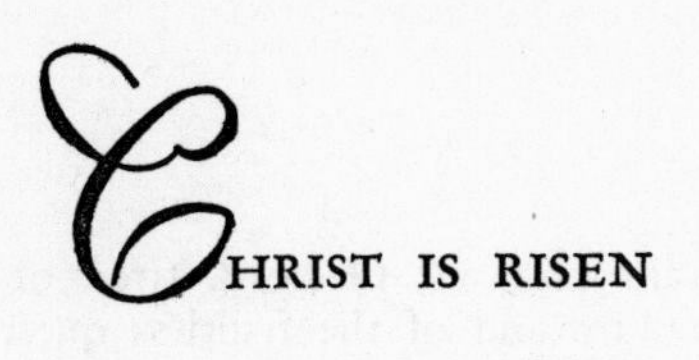
CHRIST IS RISEN

A PRAYER

Grant unto us, O Lord, tired of our own failure and of the fruitless quest for life's meaning, to accept the gift of thy companionship. Fill our lives with new joy and a new sense of power, and with thee may we take courage and begin again. Through us, as through thy men of old, may thy purpose be fulfilled. Amen.

I. CHRIST IS RISEN

FOR THOUSANDS of people of every nationality in the world, Easter is the gladdest day of the whole year. In a thousand languages men will sing and say, "Christ is risen." In churches of every denomination in the world men and women will rejoice that Jesus Christ is alive.

Do you really believe that—that the Person who stood on the beach of the Sea of Galilee and called men to follow him, who offered men a new way of life, who healed their diseases and sympathized with them in their sorrows, who was put to death by the Roman authorities, is alive?

It isn't easy to realize it. On one man, a minister who had preached about him for years, the truth dawned. This is what he afterward wrote in his diary:

"Christ is alive," I said to myself. "Alive!" And then I paused: "Alive!" And then I paused again: "Alive!" Can that really be true? Living as really as I myself am? I got up and walked about repeating, "Christ is living!

Christ is living!" At first it seemed strange and hardly true, but at last it came upon me as a burst of sudden glory; yes, Christ is alive. It was to me a new discovery. I thought that all along I had believed it; but not until that moment did I feel sure about it. I then said, "My people shall know it. I shall preach it again and again until they believe it as I do now." [1]

He did, too, and there is no more important truth in the world than just that, that Jesus Christ is still alive.

How do we know that Christ is risen? Critics say, "Perhaps he wasn't really dead, or someone removed the body, or his followers indulged in a bit of wishful thinking." But, men and women, there cannot be any doubt about it. Could a person suffering from five terrible wounds, all of them involving serious loss of blood, lie in a cold grave for thirty-six hours, and then, awaking from a coma, push away a heavy stone rolled in front of the tomb entrance, and not just stagger out of the tomb, but remove the grave-clothes, procure other clothing, evade the guards, and persuade his followers that he had conquered death? He would be an invalid needing weeks of care. As to anybody removing the body, is it then so easy to dispose of a body? Seven weeks after his death his followers were preaching his resurrection to those who

[1] A. W. Dale, *Life of R. W. Dale of Birmingham*, p. 642.

put him to death. If Jews or Romans had removed the body, would they not have said so, proved it, and ended Christianity once for all? Did his own men remove it, keep the fact a secret for seven weeks, and then preach what they knew to be a lie, which anyone knowing what had been done with the body could have exposed? And did those eleven men proceed to give their lives for this lie? And is the universal Church of Christ which has now spread to all peoples and nations—is it all based on that lie?

"Perhaps," says the critic, "the body remained in the tomb, and the disciples saw a ghost." But the irrefutable evidence is that the grave was empty. Anyone who liked was invited to see the evidence. "Come, see the place where the Lord lay!" And as for ghost stories:

> It is a new thing in ghost stories which turns abject terror into flaming courage and cowards into heroes and martyrs. It drove ordinary shrinking men, like ourselves, to go shouting a message to audiences as derisive as some men are today, a message punished with stripes and crosses and red-jowled beasts, yet persisting, indomitable, on and on down the echoing centuries, until a pagan world was conquered by a handful of Jewish fishermen and a great Church raised its pinnacles to heaven to enshrine that message flung to the wind on Easter Sunday.[2]

[2] W. A. Kirkland, *Who Is This Jesus?*

Of course, if you ask me how it all happened, I don't know. I don't think anybody knows. The men who entered the tomb first were very impressed by the way the graveclothes which bound Christ's body had just collapsed as if the body had evaporated. If they had found all the spices on the floor of the cave-tomb—and there were a hundred pounds weight of embalming spices between the folds of the grave-clothes—they would have thought that somebody had rifled the tomb and stolen the body. But the graveclothes had just collapsed, and the turban which had been wrapped round his head was still lying on its side. It was the way those graveclothes and the turban were lying that convinced Peter and John that he had risen. As the Fourth Gospel says, "They saw [the graveclothes] and believed."

After all, though we rightly seek to understand everything that happens in this old world, there have been other occasions when things have happened without anyone ever understanding why or how. For example, once this old earth was red hot. Its scenery must have been like the inside of a furnace. After a long period of cooling that mysterious thing we call life appeared. Why? No one knows. How? No one knows. No one watching this earth from Mars—if for a moment we imagine anyone able to do so—could possibly have prophesied that when the world was cool enough life would appear. You can stress, if you like, the long centuries that passed, but time by itself doesn't create life. You might stick an old poker in the earth, and, if you could, leave it there for a hundred years, but it would not become a tree. It would still be a lifeless old rusty poker. If God can produce life on a planet once red-hot, is it silly to believe that he can raise from the dead his own dearly loved Son? Who are we to say what is possible when God is at work?

Now, no one thought Christ would really rise from the dead in that way, or his own men would have been full of joyous expectancy. They would have been waiting round that tomb in which Jesus was buried. But, on the contrary, they were shut up in a room in Jerusalem, with the doors barred for fear, and the greatest proof of the Resurrection is the complete change in their attitude. Instead of being frightened and depressed and in abject despair, once they were convinced they were triumphantly shouting the glorious news to anyone who would listen.

Just like the inexplicable, unforseeable emergence of life on this old earth, here we have another inexplicable thing happening. No one knows how or why in either case. But no one can, in either case, deny the facts. They doubtless fit into the framework of law somehow, but no one knows how.

Henry Drummond said:

> What if it should be perfectly normal for a sinless man to rise from the dead, as it is for a sinful man to remain in the grave? What if perfect nearness to the great Author and Sustainer of all should give a man power over all the tragic forces of nature and time?

We know a tiny bit about the power of mind over body. If Christ, as I believe, is the Son of God, what may have been the power of *his* mind over *his* body?

Just as no one now can deny the fact of life on this earth, so no one can deny that the story of the risen Christ has been preached now to the men of all nations and is being increasingly accepted by them and acted upon. Many of them do not *understand* the Resurrection any more than we do, but Jesus Christ to them is a personal Friend. They are as much his disciples as were Peter and John. They are pledged to try to follow him in their daily lives and so to carry out his will that evil shall be banished; greed and selfishness, poverty and misery, be done away; and a new world emerge in which all men shall be his men, loving and serving one another. What if the risen Christ is the clue for which all the world is groping? What if the power of the risen Christ—far greater than atomic power both to break down and to build up—is the only power that can save us? Do consider this one thought. If Christianity is a lie and built on lies, if Christ never rose, if all that he means is just of the same stuff as a beautiful dream of long ago, let us, in truth's name, forget it and get down to brass tacks and see what we can make of life without bothering any more with Jesus Christ. But if he is the Son of God and alive, you cannot leave him out; and every scheme for making a new world, every political program, or economic plan, or scheme of reformation which leads us away from him, from his purposes and his spirit, leads us nearer to disaster. Either he was right, or he was wrong. If he was wrong, forget him. If he was right, *is* right; if he is alive to be followed, and if he is still able to guide men, then, for the love of God and man, follow him, for he *must reign.*

Jesus Christ is alive! He is as near to you as he was to Peter when they were fishing on the Sea of Galilee. And he offers that same transforming friendship which is the very heart of the gospel. He is still alive! Still an available Friend! Still able to change the whole world!

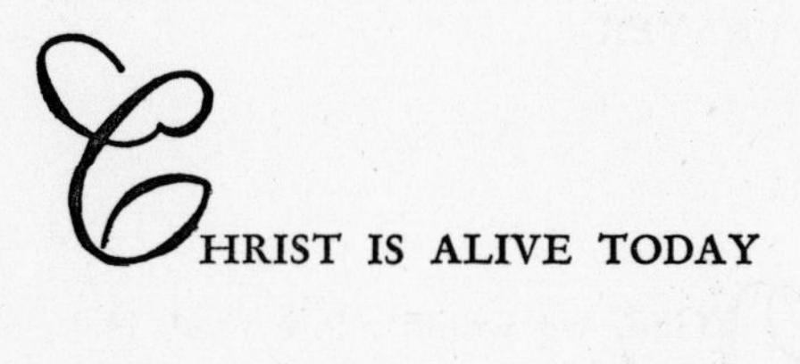
CHRIST IS ALIVE TODAY

A PRAYER

O God, we would adore thee. Help us sincerely to worship thee so that our consciences may be quickened by the thought of thy holiness, our minds fed by thy truth, our imagination quickened by thy beauty, our hearts opened by thy love, our wills strengthened by the thought of thy purposes, our whole being dedicated to thy glory, who dost reign with the Son and the Holy Ghost, one God, world without end. Amen.

II. CHRIST IS ALIVE TODAY

I WONDER what you consider to be the very essence of the Christian religion. In these days when there is so much controversy going on about what people ought to believe, it seems to me very important that each of us should think as clearly and simply as he can about what really *is* fundamental. And, of course, there is not much sense in trying to make yourself believe a thing because other people tell you you *ought* to believe. You can believe only something which appears to *you* to be true. If you've tried it out and it works, or if you've seen it work out in other people, so much the better.

In religion we have to walk by faith. We cannot produce the same kind of evidence as the scientist, though in my opinion the conclusions we come to about the fundamentals of religion are just as trustworthy as those of science.

And what *is* faith? A schoolboy said, "Faith is believing what you know to be untrue!" Many people's faith is an effort to believe on the authority of another. My definition would be that faith is an attitude of complete sincerity in regard to the trend of all the available evidence—a sincerity both of thought and of action.

And to me the fundamental and basic truth of the Christian religion is that Jesus Christ is God manifested in the flesh; that he not only lived a truly human life many years ago and was cruelly put to death, but rose again from the dead and *is still alive in our midst today*.

I emphasize those last words because I honestly do not think there is any fact in the world more important than that.

You see, when he lived in the flesh among men, it was not what he said and did which changed men's lives, wonderful and beautiful though his words and deeds were. It was the very fact of his friendship. If you could live with him for a week, or even a day, I am certain that all that is good and noble in you would be strengthened and all that is bad would wither and die. Now that is what happened in Galilee. Men and women were changed. Simple peasants and fishermen and housewives became saints. The only explanation that the world could find to account for the change is very simply stated in the New Testament: "They have been with Jesus."

Suppose he *is* still alive. Suppose we can still make contact with him. Don't you see what a tremendous claim Christianity makes and what wonderfully good news this is? It means that human nature *can* be changed. Why, it's the belief that nothing can change human nature that ruins *all* our plans for progress.

If Christ is still alive and in our midst and can still do in the world what he did in the days of his flesh, it's the most tremendous fact in the world.

I believe the evidence is overwhelming that he *is* alive and that he *is* at work; that man has never been left desolate and, best of all, that we can make contact with him. If half a dozen signposts, with the name of the same village painted on them, all point one way, then sincerity in regard to the evidence compels belief that the village exists, even though we have never been there. And what with the gospel story, the testimony of the martyrs, the lives of the saints, the changed lives some of us have seen, and the advance of missionary work in other lands, it is incredible that Christianity is an immense delusion and that it is based upon a lie.

If you have followed me so far, you will be asking, "Well, are we to think of Christ as a kind of ghostly presence going about with us?"

I don't think so. Between the Resurrection and the Ascension, Christ taught his disciples to think of him without the need of eyes, ears, and touch. And they did that. Do you realize that when he ascended, they never felt he had gone? They never said good-by or felt as we do when we say good-by at the station to someone whom we dearly love. Every day they felt he was a kind of personal energy within them, reinforcing their personality from inside.

Everybody knows a little psychology these days. Everybody knows that his real "self" is made up of thinking, feeling, and willing. Nowadays Christ does not often "appear" to people, but he visits their thoughts; and then their thinking about other people and about life and the world is broad and noble and true. He visits their feelings; and then they find they can get on better with difficult folk. They are more tolerant of people with a different outlook; they feel a deep sense of joy and serenity, and are not so easily ruffled and made hectic. He visits their will; and they are not concerned with just their own private and selfish ambitions. They *hate* the evils in the world that make men miserable and deprive them of happiness and the means to live a full life, and they determine in his name to build a new world where God's good gifts can be shared among the men of all nations and his will be done on earth.

Christ comes now in his Spirit to men and women at such a depth of personality that they are often unconscious that he has been there, but in the depths of being he is doing the same thing that he did when he lived in Palestine. He is changing men's lives, altering their reactions to life. A girl was converted in my former church in Leeds, and after some months she came back to my room after a service and said, "It's no good. Religion doesn't work. I'm just as bad-tempered as ever. I'm giving it up."

I won't bore you with what I said to her. The strange thing was that she had not been gone ten minutes when her father, who did not know she had been to church that evening, came in and put down a generous donation on the table for the work of my Men's Samaritan League among the poor. I said, "What's this for?"

"I'm giving you that," he said, "because since my daughter started coming here, she's not only a different girl, but my home's a different place. The whole atmosphere's different."

No! We don't realize how different we are and how changed we can still be. But if you are fed up with life and fed up with yourself, bored with your job and with nearly everybody you meet, give Jesus Christ a chance. If he really is still alive—as I and millions of others believe—he can still do what he used to do: completely change our lives.

Well, what are we to do? The answer is that we

have to make a little adventure of prayer. After all, we take care to keep a human friendship in good repair if we value it very much, don't we? A closer walk with God, that's what we need.

Why not try this experiment? Start ten minutes earlier for work and drop into a church; or if that's too much, drop in on your way home; or if that's too much, go off alone to some quiet place and reserve a time, if it's only once a week, when you keep an appointment with Christ. If it's hard to think of him as a spirit within you, then imagine him as a human person. If it helps, think of a young Man with smiling, sun-tanned face, standing on the shore of the Sea of Galilee, and imagine that you are there talking to him and listening to him.

But do make the experiment and keep on with it for six months, and don't test results by your feelings. You may *feel* no different. You may feel like throwing the thing up. But keep it up and leave results to him, and if he asks you to do something, even something hard, do it, for he knows what he is doing. He can change your life. You see, he is the Saviour of the world.

Here is a quotation from Schweitzer:

He comes to us as One unknown, without a name, as of old by the lakeside he came to those who knew him not.

He speaks to us the same word, "Follow thou me," and sets us to the task which he has to fulfill for our time. He commands. And to those who obey him, whether they be wise or simple, he will reveal himself in the toils, the conflicts, the sufferings which they shall pass through in his fellowship, and, as an ineffable mystery, they shall learn in their own experience who he is.

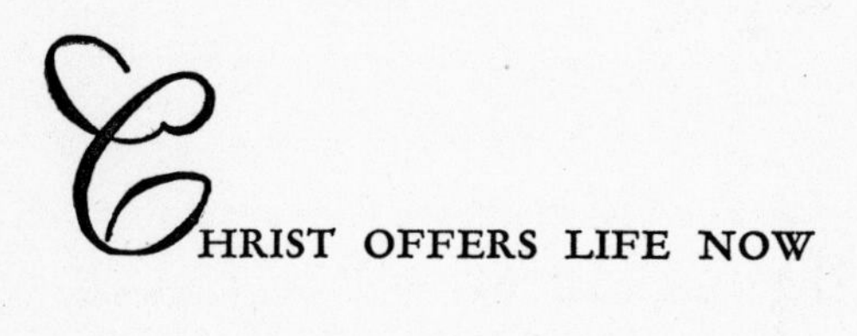

CHRIST OFFERS LIFE NOW

A PRAYER

O God, the Father of us all, forgive us for everything in our lives which is contrary to thy will. Help us to begin again each morning, and, by thy grace, to have done with everything that hinders thy purposes, hurts others, and spoils our own lives. May we know now the sense of spiritual power that follows thy pardon and our decision to follow thee. Send us out in thy strength to fulfill thy purposes for us and for the world. Through Jesus Christ our Lord. Amen.

III. CHRIST OFFERS LIFE NOW

IF YOU get a chance sometime, read John Masefield's narrative poem, *The Everlasting Mercy*. It's as easy to read as your evening paper, and much more exciting. It tells how Saul Kane, a boozing, boasting blackguard, is confronted by a gentle Quakeress, who wins him to a new way of life. He blunders out into the light of the early morning, and this is what he says:

> O glory of the lighted mind.
> How dead I'd been, how dumb, how blind.
> The station brook, to my new eyes,
> Was babbling out of Paradise,
> The waters rushing from the rain
> Were singing Christ has risen again.
> I thought all earthly creatures knelt
> From rapture of the joy I felt.
> The narrow station-wall's brick ledge,
> The wild hop withering in the hedge,
> The lights in huntsman's upper storey,
> Were parts of an eternal glory,

Were God's eternal garden flowers.
I stood in bliss at this for hours.[1]

What *is* this new life found through Christ? Is it just a fancy of religious people? Is it a fact? Is it to be found only by some people who are religiously inclined? Is it for everybody, even though its forms vary?

Whatever it is, I think, deep down, thousands want it. People are fed up with life, at sixes and sevens with themselves, wondering what life means–indeed, whether it means anything at all.

It looks as if there *is* a new way of living, doesn't it, whatever we call it? It isn't just for blackguards either. It's for respectable people like us, who never think of ourselves as sinners, who would never get intoxicated or steal money, but who quite cheerfully steal someone's good name and are intoxicated with our own self-importance. And the New Testament says this new life is so different from the life most people live that it's like going from darkness to light, from prison to freedom, and even from death to life.

Do you think these metaphors are exaggerated? Let's look at them.

[1] Copyright 1911 by John Masefield. Used by permission of The Macmillan Co.

DARKNESS TO LIGHT

Here is a picture which I should like you to have at the back of your mind. It is midnight in some tropical and strange land. You are in the midst of dense jungle, and you are lost. You stumble along blindly, unable to find any path. You trip in the undergrowth and fall against the trunks of great trees that soar up into the night above your head. The bushes whip your face. The thorns tear your clothing and your flesh. Panic fills your mind. You realize that it is no good even trying to climb one of the trees, for you would see nothing at midnight in the jungle.

Then, very gradually, the first glimmer of a dawn seeps through the darkness of the forest. You climb one of the easiest trees you can find, and you get high enough to note your bearings. There is the sea to your right hand. There is a great range of mountains to your left. You know now the general lie of the track, and through the early dawn you move with certainty until at last you find a pathway. You are not at the end of your journey, but you are at the end of your wandering. You cannot find rest for your body, but already you have found rest for your mind. The pathway is still only a track, and you may be at only the beginning of a long journey, but you are on the path and going the right way. Because darkness turned to light, you have found the way home, and you are saved. Being saved is finding the path home. A man isn't lost merely because he hasn't *arrived* home. No one is lost who knows the way home.

PRISON TO FREEDOM

Then, says the New Testament, to find the new life in Christ is like passing from prison to freedom. I don't know whether you have ever visited anybody in prison. When I have done so, I have been distressed at the continual clanging of steel doors, the sound of keys on a chain round the warder's waist, the clinking as he walks along, the sound of the key in the lock. You go to see a poor fellow who, in the eyes of God, has probably done no worse a thing than we have done many a time, but doors must be unlocked and locked again, slammed with a noise that goes right through you, until you come face to face with the man who apparently needs all these terrible precautions and who is shut away from society.

What must it be to such a person when a door slams behind him for the last time and he is face to face with freedom?

DEATH TO LIFE

Here is the strongest metaphor of all. The New Testament says that to find the new way of life in Christ is like passing from death to life. It is as though the New Testament writers cannot find language strong enough to carry their meaning.

I was reading recently the story of some British explorers who were carrying out excavations among the tombs of Egypt. They came to one which had remained shut for three thousand years. When they opened it, they found an exquisitely carved coffin of a little child, and over it this inscription: "Oh my life, my love, my little one, would God I had died for thee!" The explorers uncovered their heads, and then stepped from the darkness of the tomb into the blazing sunshine of the Egyptian noon. They sealed the tomb and went quietly away. How final a thing seems death! What must it have been like to have been with Christ when death gave place to life, so that, at his word, the face lighted up again, the arms were outstretched to embrace the loved one and the eyes were eloquent with recognition? We cannot conceive a more tremendous thing to say than that to find the new life in Christ is to pass from death unto life.

Whether you think the metaphors are exaggerated or not, the first part of each isn't, is it? The word "darkness" is not exaggerated, nor the word "prison," nor the word "death."

Darkness! Do you not think that this will become known in history as the generation of men who were lost in a great darkness? The picture of a jungle at night. Is it an exaggeration? I don't think so. Show me one leader in the world today who knows where he is going, who has found the road which will lead humanity where it wants to be and who is stepping out on it with confidence, who feels there is something ahead worth striving for and who is leading others to strive for it, manfully and successfully. Who *will* lead our poverty-stricken humanity and guide it into the way of peace? There is no exaggeration about darkness.

Is there any exaggeration about the word "prison"? Do you not find the men and women around you held down by chains you cannot see, but whose rattle and jangle you hear from time to time, especially when an impulse stirs within them to have done with imprisonment altogether? Are you yourself the prisoner of certain habits and of certain thoughts, of certain compromises, of certain selfish ways of life? Are you becoming a slave to comfort and to your own pleasure, never thinking sacrificially of your brother, never feeling any obligation to serve the community at cost to yourself, never lifting your eyes above the near horizon of your own interests and desire for success? How many of us are the slaves of our own selfishness? Shut up in prison for life!

A free world requires free men. You cannot run a free world with slaves. There is not the slightest doubt that God's plan for his world is that it shall be a world-wide brotherhood of free men, all of them sons; and perhaps it might not be a bad thing if we shelved some of our blueprints that show how cleverly we can work out schemes and bent every energy to make sure that those who are going to work them are themselves free men. No! There is no exaggeration in the word "prison."

Is there any exaggeration in the word "death"? I am sorry if this message is depressing to some, but if it stabs you, it may do you the service of stabbing you awake. I believe most intensely in the survival of the soul after death. But when Jesus spoke about death and life, he did not mean by "death" physical extinction, or by the word "life" mere survival. He meant by death the suffocation of everything by which the soul of man lives in a full, spiritual sense. Many, no doubt, think that it is unfair of the Christian minister to talk as though only Christian people were really alive. But there is a very true sense in which only those who are in a living relationship with God through Jesus Christ merit what *Jesus* meant by the word "life." I know that there are a lot of jolly pagans around. The story of the prodigal son is about one of them. It was a story Jesus told about a most attractive young fellow. "A jolly good sort," we should call him, "a sport." And off he goes to have a good time.

Nothing mean about *him.* The sort of boy who gets on with everybody, ever so much nicer to know than some of the people who hang around the churches, and much more human than ministers and deacons and elders and what not. What if he did travel to other countries and have a good time? Why shouldn't he? Youth must sow its wild oats. And nobody could *help* liking him. *He* would never do anybody a dirty trick.

But wait a minute! This is not my story. It is a story Jesus told. And Jesus said, "He was dead."

Finally he came back, ragged, hungry, and disheveled, a little bleary at the eyes, with a shifty, shady look about him. But he came home, and then the old father said, "This my son was dead, and is alive again; he was lost, and is found." The claim of Christianity is that Christ has power to overcome death by a new life which he alone gives.

I asked the question whether the metaphors were exaggerated. They are not exaggerated if Christ can do what is claimed for him. Do you really think he can? If there is anybody wishing that it were true, but who is still a little incredulous, let me speak to you. If there is somebody who would have believed it thirty years ago, but who now feels too old to change, let me speak to you. If there is somebody who has tried and tried and tried again and has not the heart to try yet once more, let me speak to you. Let me remind you of those three favorite words of Jesus—"least," "last," and "lost." For he said that the least should be the greatest, and the last should be first, and the lost should be found. My friends, the New Testament is a lie if Jesus cannot do what is claimed for him. The existence of the Church is built on an illusion if men and women cannot be changed, whatever their age, whatever they have done, whatever their past history of failure and frustration may be. The sacrifices of the martyrs and the lives of the saints are records of neurotic illness if Jesus Christ cannot save men and women. Some of the greatest heroes and heroines in the world have been fooled if it is not true. Some of the great mass movements of history and the great reformations have been as meaningless as the froth on the surface of the sea if his power to change life is not a fact more solid than the mountains, more firmly established than the stars.

I, speaking to you, know that this is true. He has not done with me yet, but he has made a beginning, and I know that without him I should be lost and life would be meaningless. If you will offer yourself to him, then, perhaps slowly, as with some of us, perhaps quickly, as with others, he can change your life. He can lift you from darkness into light, from the slavery of evil to the happy relationship of a son or daughter, and from the hard grip of death to the joy of life. And you know what to do. Listen to what that young man said: "I will arise and go to my father, and will say unto him, Father, I have sinned against heaven, and before thee, and am no more worthy to be called thy son." God will receive you. God will understand you. God will know what to do with you. God will tell you where to begin.

CHRIST OFFERS LIFE HEREAFTER

PRAYERS

Lift our eyes, we beseech thee, O risen Christ, to wide horizons; above the noise and strife and tumult of this present world. Help us to remember that we are immortal spirits. We must be trained in this hard school we call the world and do our best to remake it according to thy will. But light in our hearts again the knowledge that we belong to an eternal world of love and joy and peace. Help us to live worthily of our destiny and, at last, reunited with those who have gone before us, see thee in thy beauty, and worship thee the ever-living, ever-loving God. For thy name's sake. Amen.

We lift up our hearts in prayer to thee, O God, for those who have been separated by death from their dear ones. Comfort them with the truth that love is immortal, that death is only a horizon, and a horizon is only the limit of our sight. Lift us up that we may see farther; cleanse our eyes that we may see more clearly; draw us closer to thyself, O thou who dost gather the dead and the living in thine all-embracing love. Prepare us for that further life where thou and thine own are one, for evermore. Through Jesus Christ our Lord. Amen.

IV. CHRIST OFFERS LIFE HEREAFTER

I WANT to talk to you in this chapter about life after death. My own opinion is that everybody *survives* death, but Christianity offers something more than mere survival. It offers something worth calling *life*.

Will you imagine for a moment that two men go to a classical concert? The first—we'll call him Murray—is a musician to the fingertips: trained in music, able to play brilliantly, able to enter fully into every part of the concert. The second—we'll call him Smith—is a friend of Murray's and goes to the concert only to please his friend. He is bored with music. He does not admit it, but, frankly, it means nothing at all to him. He likes a melody that goes with a swing all right, but most of the music at a high-brow concert leaves him cold.

At the concert Murray really *lives*. He is in a world of wonder and delight, "thrilled to bits," as we say. Smith is musically just alive, that's all. They sit together, but between them there is a great gulf. Smith cannot cross it all in a moment and be where Murray is. Murray's long training, hours of study, and laborious practice have enabled him to revel fully in this wonderful musical treat. Poor Smith is feeling horribly out of it. He cannot respond to music, and *at the concert* music is all there is to respond to.

I wonder if dying is rather like going to that concert. We pass to a spiritual world where the only enjoyment is spiritual. We all *survive*, I think. But whether we fully live and revel in the afterlife will surely depend on the extent to which, on this side of the grave, we have trained our spiritual faculties, just as the enjoyment of the people at a concert depends on the extent to which they have developed the power to make a musical response. I never think of heaven and hell as two *places*. I think it must be hell to be in heaven and not be able to enter into its delights—like being at an endless concert and being deaf, or like being at a banquet and having no appetite.

We do not use the word "saint" much now, but the saints are the people who make it easier to be good, who make us more eager to develop our spiritual capacities. So let's thank God for them and remember those—some of them our own dear ones—who are now enjoying the delights of heaven.

People have said to me, "That idea of life after death, you know, is a bit of wishful thinking. You don't want to be snuffed out, so you just kid yourself that you won't. But that's not an argument." They say, "When the candle is used up or broken, the light goes out, and when the body dies, you are done for. What's the answer to that?"

Well, that's not an argument either. It's a statement about a candle, not necessarily an argument about the soul of man. And it's a poor statement for the purpose because, according to Sir Oliver Lodge, the light of the candle is still somewhere in the universe and that is what the candle was made for. The body of man was created to express his spirit, and there is no logic in the argument that because his body is broken the light of his spirit ceases to exist.

Think of your radio as your body and the music as your soul or spirit. The radio is made to express the music. I believe that the body was made to express the soul. Even if your radio is damaged or broken, the music is still there. When the body is smashed up, the soul still exists. The analogy goes farther. You could go and get another and a better radio and express the music through that. Christianity teaches that when this body perishes, we still have a spiritual body—another radio, another way of expressing our soul. Ask yourself whether that is only a statement about a radio or an analogy which carries truth. Ask yourself whether we are doing a bit of wishful thinking or building our thoughts on the nature of God and man.

As for wishful thinking, what a silly way we have of using that phrase! Of course, if we pretend a thing is true *only* because we *want* it to be true, we are foolish. But we now use the phrase and hurl it at one another as though a thing *cannot* be true if we wish it were true; that to wish it were true proves it isn't. What nonsense that is! If my child is ill, my mind is full of "wishful thinking" that he will recover. Does that prevent his recovery or make it impossible? And remember, when you are thinking about *God*, you cannot wish anything better than the truth. A lot of things we want are not good enough to be true. But nothing is too good to be true. It cannot be if God is wholly good and in full charge of his universe.

One lovely spring morning I found a lark's nest in a field, and I held in my hand a lark's egg. Within that little brown egg there was life. It was a very shut-in life. Yet what promise there was of a wider life that would begin when the little bird inside broke the shell and escaped! Within the egg were wings. Within the egg was the apparatus–not yet fully developed–which would be capable of producing the lovely song of the lark as, later, it flew up into the sunlight of a summer morning.

I feel that there is an illustration of something that is true about man. No one can prove it mathematically, of course. But I cannot believe that the universe is purposeless and meaningless. The structure of the bird within the egg is meaningless unless there will come the chance to fly and to sing. What is the point of producing powers which can never be used? Wings mean air to fly in. Eyes mean something to see. A throat means a chance one day to sing.

Don't you feel sometimes as though this life is meaningless unless there is another? If man perishes at death, then the universe is as irrational as it would be if every bird died at the moment of hatching out. Some people never really *live* here at all. They never have a chance to express all their possibilities. They live a cramped life, full of frustration and pain, and as shut in as a bird inside the egg, but they *could* live if they had the chance. The apparatus is there. All of us have faculties we never fully use, longings we never fully realize—yes, and friendships that surely death cannot cut off forever. Those friendships are made of love, the final "stuff" of the universe. If anything is strong enough to withstand the shock of death, love is. I have not the slightest doubt in my own mind that, for those who love, reunion after death is certain.

We have all noticed that in many matters it is the word of the expert which convinces us. If ever you had a dear one very ill, and consulted a specialist, I hope you did not argue with the specialist. You didn't say, "Have you thought of this? Do you think it might be that?" You were out of your depth about these medical matters, and you took his word. Similarly, I would not argue with an astronomer as to how far one star is from another. I am out of my depth. I take his word. If he doesn't know, no one does. I would not argue with Einstein about relativity. I'm right out of my depth. If he doesn't know, no one does. Somebody once said to Mrs. Einstein, "Do *you* know all about relativity?" Smilingly, she replied, "No, but I know my husband, and I know he can be trusted."

Now, is there any expert on the subject we are talking about—life after death? I think there is! I mean Jesus Christ. If he does not know, nobody does. When he was talking about the God of Abraham, Isaac, and Jacob, who had been dead for centuries, he added this: "And God is not the God of the dead but of the living; for *all* live unto him." Best of all, when Jesus hung on the cross next to a dying thief—not a man who had qualified by his character for heaven—he did *not* say, "Well, I *hope* we shall meet again." He said, "Today shalt thou be with me in paradise." Hold on to that! Either Jesus was *certain*, or he was not being honest with that poor wretch dying on the cross next his own. He did *not* say, "I've got an idea that we *may* meet again after death." He, the Expert of experts in all matters of religion, said, "It is so."

Well, frankly, that convinces me. For I believe, as millions do, that that was not only the opinion of a great Teacher, but a revelation of God.

So don't be afraid of death. He who knew how to bring us into this world and so arranged birth that we should be received into a home, with loving arms around us from the moment of birth, will not fail to bring us into the next world with all the love and comfort we need. I've seen many people die. Many die in an unconscious and blessed sleep. For the most part the rest, unless they have been the enemies of God or have some fears of a psychopathological origin, find the actual experience of dying a wonderfully happy experience, even if their faith and understanding are pathetically small. Dying appears to be like waking up after a long, dark, stormy night of pain to find the sunshine streaming through the windows and all the pain and terror gone.

Do you know these lines of John Oxenham about a patient who was terrified of death?

> Shapeless and grim,
> A Shadow dim
> O'erhung the ways
> And darkened all my days.
> And all who saw,

With bated breath,
Said, "It is death!"

And I, in weakness
Slipping towards the Night,
In sore affright
Looked up. And lo!—
No Spectre grim,
But just a dim
Sweet face,
A sweet high mother-face,
A face like Christ's own mother's face
Alight with tenderness
And grace.

"Thou art not Death," I cried;—
For Life's supremest fantasy
Had never *thus* envisaged Death to me;—
"Thou art not Death, the End!"

In accents winning
Came the answer: "*Friend,*
There is no Death!
I am the Beginning,
—Not the End!"[1]

[1] "The Shadow." Used by permission of Miss Erica Oxenham.

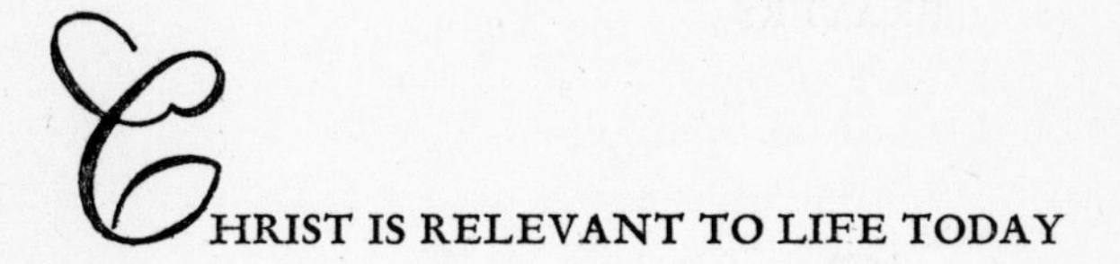

CHRIST IS RELEVANT TO LIFE TODAY

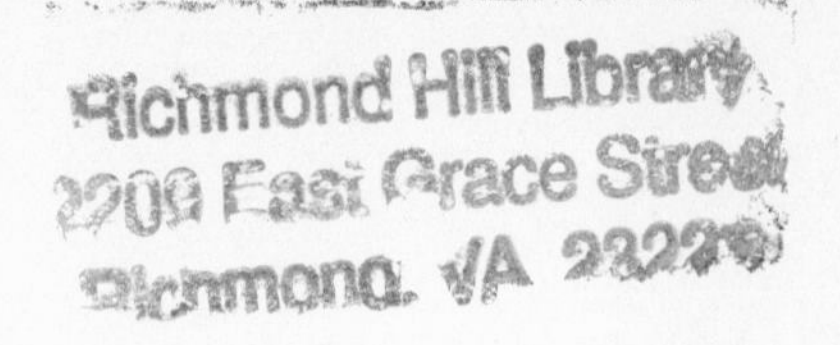

PRAYERS

Grant us, O God, a vision of our land, fair as she might be; a land of justice, where none shall prey on others; a land of plenty, where vice and poverty shall cease to fester; a land of brotherhood, where success shall be founded on service, and honor be given to worth alone; a land of peace, where order need no longer rest on force, but on the love of all for their land, the great mother of the common life and welfare. Hear thou, O Lord, the silent prayer of all our hearts, as in city, town, and village we pledge our time and strength and thought to hasten the day of her coming beauty and righteousness. Through Jesus Christ our Lord. Amen.

God of our life, there are days when the burdens we carry chafe our shoulders and weigh us down; when the road seems dreary and endless, the skies gray and threatening; when our lives have no music in them, and our hearts are lonely and our souls have lost their courage. Flood the path with light, we beseech thee; turn our eyes to where the skies are full of promise; tune our hearts to brave music; give us the sense of comradeship with heroes and saints of every age; and so quicken our spirits that we may be able to encourage the souls of all who journey with us on the road of life, to thy honor and glory. Through Jesus Christ our Lord. Amen.

V. CHRIST IS RELEVANT TO LIFE TODAY

THERE are some people who are not a bit hostile to religion, but they just won't think it has anything to do with the problems we are all facing just now. They suppose that religious people get *something* out of it, comfort in hours of sorrow, and what is vaguely called *uplift* at a good service, and so on. But religion to them is the interest of the few, like music or golf or gardening. "Nice if you like it," as one might say. To them, those of us who keep on talking about it as if it mattered are, frankly, rather a bore.

Now, if Christ were only a teacher who lived long ago in Palestine, said and did some very beautiful things, and then was cruelly put to death; if all the talk about him rising again and living on in the world as a Spirit—if all that is legend, well, although we should all be much better off if we heeded those words and copied those deeds, yet we should have no right to keep talking as if he mattered vitally now.

He might not be what we call relevant to our life today.

But, you see, many of us really *do* believe that what the Church so definitely teaches is the truth; namely, that he was and is God—as much of God as could be expressed in a human life without destroying its humanity. If *that* is true, when he speaks, we are listening to God, and when he acts significantly, we are watching God at work.

And if *that* is true, we had better stop and think hard, for it means that Christ not only is relevant, but is the clue to the problems we are all facing. His way is God's way, and no other way will work. For do remember this: We exist for God. God doesn't exist for us. The world exists for *his* purposes, not ours. And the minute we try to twist life and make it serve *our* purposes instead of his, we get into trouble. An automobile was made for roads, not swamps. And if you drive it off the road into a swamp—well, it sticks, and there you are. It won't do what it wasn't made to do—nor will life. Life will work out only one way, and that is God's way. If a man, or a society, or a nation, chooses a different way, however successful it may appear for a time, and however plausible may be the arguments of those who lead us along it, if it is not God's way, we find either the road ends in a precipice, or else there is a notice, "No Thoroughfare This Way," and we have to come back. As everybody knows, to come back along a road that was downhill is to find it is uphill.

Let me illustrate what I mean by getting onto the wrong road. You have all heard about what is called "free love." Haven't you heard people argue like this: "Why remain loyal to the marriage bond? Why not have promiscuous sex adventures with others willing to travel the same path? Realize how dangerous it is to suppress your instincts. Have a good time sexually while you may. Don't be cramped by the conventions of stuffy Victorians, or held down by artificial moral systems imposed to imprison and curtail your liberties." And so on, and so on. Well, I have been in the Christian ministry thirty years and have seen many individuals take that road. But I have never known one person who found the promised liberty. The goods advertised are never delivered. The promised freedom is never found. What I *have* seen is those individuals coming back slowly and painfully along the broad road they thought was going to lead to life, and finding that what was downhill then is a very steep uphill way now. Others have never come back at all morally. They have gone over the precipice at the end of that road. All who travel a way that is not God's way find self-loathing and remorse, frequently a shattered body, often a shattered mind and nerves, and always a shattered soul.

So often what is true for the individual is true for the nation, and here there are plenty of illustrations. Do you remember how a proud Italy—Italy who brought Abyssinia into the League of Nations—tested the League and found that its members were not prepared to stand by the pledges they made to Abyssinia? As soon as Italy saw that the League of Nations did not mean business, she invaded Abyssinia, fighting natives and half-civilized peoples with the poison gas which she never *dared* to use in the Second World War against civilized nations, who could have answered her with similar measures. There was a time when the exiled Emperor of Abyssinia made pilgrimage to the Holy City and knelt at the traditional site of Calvary to ask the will of God and find out God's way for his nation. At that moment Mussolini, the boastful hyena, was barking from the balcony of the Palazzio Venezzia in Rome and appeared to himself to be a successful conqueror instead of the despicable and cowardly tyrant he really was. But history has judged between them. The nation, like the individual, never gets away with evil-doing, and every road (even when it is called by the most high-sounding names) which is not the way of God for a nation ends in disaster, as Italy has found to her cost.

Condemning others is easy. Let us look at the life of England. I am not a pacifist even now, and I realize that the sin of the world can drive the best-intentioned nation to the dreadful dilemma of having to do wrong, a dilemma in which she is not free to choose between black and white but between two grays. And I must still admit that, to my mind, the lesser evil was to fight the Nazi tyranny and break it. The alternative would have been that the slime of Nazism would have been smeared across all Europe, our children would have been denied the Christian faith, and even more millions would have suffered the bestial atrocities which we came to recognize as the mark of the Nazi beast.

But when all that has been said, we simply must realize that a great nation cannot spend its energies for six years trying to kill people and ennoble its soul thereby. Obliteration bombing—which Britain so hotly condemned when the Germans tried it in earlier days—is not an ideal preparation for the spiritual leadership of the world. A nation cannot complacently assent to Hiroshima and Nagasaki with scarcely a protest, and emerge spiritually purified. Whoever may be to blame, a nation cannot administer the British

Zone in Germany in the manner in which that zone has been administered; it cannot hold German prisoners from their homes and their loved ones for over two years after hostilities have ceased; it cannot so sink in its moral standards that people steal the electric light bulbs out of railway coaches, and so on, and then expect that as a result it will be spiritually prepared to be the instrument in the hand of God by which his purposes in the world are carried out.

The confusion, the sense of frustration, the bewilderment, and the darkness that are upon us are the moral judgments of God, the effects of sin. People actually say, "Why doesn't God *do* something? Why doesn't God speak?" But what else, in heaven's name, do they want? What voice from heaven, what miracle of divine revelation, what writing on the wall, could speak more powerfully than our present confusion? God is not the kind of person who arbitrarily hands out penalties, either to the individual who takes the law into his own hands or to the nation that does so. And if you still hold the outworn heresy that God rewards a man with cancer for not saying his prayers, or lets a baby die to teach a woman to go to church, it is time you threw over that silly heresy which Jesus stamped on two thousand years ago when he called disease part of the bondage of Satan (Luke 13:16).

But you cannot overthrow the fundamental truth which I indicated a moment ago. God does not hand out arbitrary penalties, either to individuals or to nations. *He does not need to.* He has so arranged life that if we act in defiance of his laws, we prove both the existence and the stern power of those laws, to our great dismay and sorrow.

Let me make that point a little more clear. People talk about *breaking* the laws of God. You cannot break them. By your disobedience in regard to them you only prove them. To take, with Chesterton, a simple case: if you walk over the edge of the cliff at the seaside, you do not break the law of gravitation. You only prove it. If you behave in a way that is opposed to the laws of health, even in ignorance, you do not break the laws of health. You only prove them. Your illness or disease proves their power. And if a nation gives way to the lures of the politicians of any party who say, "Come with us! We have the whole situation in hand. We will show you how to live so that everything will work out happily," remember that at any point at which we oppose the laws of God, we do not break his laws. We break ourselves on them. Those unchangeable laws are the expression of the divine Mind; and at the point at which we are disobedient, we suffer.

The confusion and distress in which we find ourselves are merely the eloquent witness of the laws of God's universe—physical, mental, *and* spiritual laws—to the fact that, after all, there *is* a God and that you cannot successfully pretend that there is not; that he is not asleep; that he is not a complacent old gentleman sitting in some remote place far above the stars, piously hoping that things will somehow come right some day; but that through every man's individual life, through the life of every community, through the life of every nation, run the unchangeable laws of God, stronger than granite and older than the stars. His purposes run through the texture of every life. All life is on *his* loom, and the final pattern will be what *he* wills, not what we plan. People may cease going to church, and they may cease saying their prayers; they may glibly laugh at religion, scorn its attempt to change men's lives, mock at the preachers, and follow selfish pursuits to their hearts' content, but that does not alter the fact of God or move by one hair's breadth his eternal throne. Every proud human head will be bowed before him at last. Every derisive sneer will wither, and every cynical laugh will die, when he is at last confronted in his blazing glory. And I would say to you, in his name, never forget that "the Lord God omnipotent *reigneth*," and, as the old proverb says, "He who will not heed the helm shall heed the rocks."

Who said that Jesus Christ was irrelevant in this hour of crisis? Who can really imagine that he was a pale, idyllic dreamer who said poetic things about lilies and birds, and need not be taken seriously?

I must state my own conviction that, for lack of taking him seriously, we may be at this moment watching the whole setup of Western civilization break up and perish. Men will not heed the preacher who says these things. They shrug their shoulders and laugh uneasily, as the men of Babylon laughed, and of Egypt and Greece and Rome and Mexico, and the rest of the fourteen ancient civilizations whose ruins are still being dug out of the desert sands. But, if I may put it thus, God's workshop floor is littered with the broken instruments that snapped in his hands and which he discarded because he could no longer use them. This is a solemn moment. We may be watching the whole of Western civilization, both in Europe and in America, snap in God's hands at the time when he wanted it most; but proud, boastful men, drunk with power, senseless with material success, blinded by the achievements of science, intoxicated by victory, and forgetful of the blood of the brave, forget that God does not exist for nations, but that nations exist for God, that life is not given us to play with. We are not even here to be happy. Life exists for God, and when any expression of it can no longer contribute toward his ends, it passes into the dust of the useless.

What can we do? In this hour when so many churches in their present way of life are too dead to be Christ's instrument, get into a group, or form one in your own home or church where you can meet, and thrash out these questions in the light of the Christian religion and the will of God.

Men and women, let us turn back to God in penitence; let us pledge ourselves, individually and collectively, to the cause of Christ. Let us persuade others to join us. Let us really try out the Christian way of life. We've tried everything else. And let us go forward together, with faces turned toward the dawn and eyes uplifted to the hills.